Daily Planner
for a

MWOV
MIGHTY WOMAN OF VALOUR

Thank you

for choosing the

Mighty Woman of Valour daily planner.

Your decision to buy from MWOV helps us share the gospel of
Jesus Christ with thousands of women across the world. Thank
you for helping us make a difference! We would love it if you
shared our blog with your friends so that together we can impact
the world for Jesus!

www.mightywomanofvalour.com

Publisher:
Cindy Nicolson
Email: info@mightywomanofvalour.com
www.mightywomanofvalour.com

Designer:
Laura Antonioli
Email: laurantonioli.jobs@yahoo.com

For more information, please reach out to us by email:
info@mightywomanofvalour.com
www.mightywomanofvalour.com

MIGHTY WOMAN OF VALOUR

What is a MWOV?

A Mighty Woman of Valour is one who chooses to spend time with her Creator. She takes time to listen for His voice and then acts on what He says by faith. *(James 1:22)*

She is Bold, Fearless, Courageous, Creative and is Successful at all she puts her hand to. Why? Because she *Believes the Promises* that God gives her in His Word. She writes it down, speaks it and lives by it. She shares the love of Jesus with others and prays for their salvation.

She could be single, married, divorced, a home-maker, an entrepreneur or an employee. She could be a mom, a wife, daughter, sister, any ethnicity & from any country - in fact you can add any label you wish to add. First and foremost however, she is *Loved, Chosen and Redeemed* and is the daughter of the Most High Living God.

That woman is YOU.

You are a *MIGHTY WOMAN OF VALOUR.*

(Prov 31:10-31)

www.mightywomanofvalour.com

THIS BOOK BELONGS TO

Name & Surname _____

Address: _____

_____

Mobile: _____

Email: _____

Daily Declarations

I Am The Daughter Of The Most High Living God. Jesus Is My Saviour & The Holy Spirit Is My Helper & Best Friend.

I Am Loved, Bold, Courageous & Kind. I Fear No Evil For I Know Who I Am In Christ.

I Am Thankful For All God's Promises Which Are Yes & Amen.

My Family Is Blessed & They Call Me Blessed.

Daily, My Soul (my mind, will, emotions) is Restored & Refreshed With God's Peace. His Mercies Are New Everyday.

I Am More Than A Conqueror In Christ & Challenges Have No Hold Over Me. I Am Above & Not Beneath.

I Live In Divine Health & Life. My Body Is Strong. I Am Energetic & Motivated & I Weigh My Ideal Weight.

All My Needs Are Met & I Lack Nothing. Because I Am A Giver At Heart, God Supplies All My Needs According To His Riches In Glory By Christ Jesus.

I Have What God Says I Have. I Can Do What God Says I Can Do. Nothing Is Impossible For Me Because I Believe & I Act On His Word By Faith.

I Am Successful In All I Do, Including My Work. My Business Is A Thriving Success, All To God's Glory.

I Can Do All Things Through Christ Who Strengthens Me.

I Am Who God Says I Am, In Jesus Name.

I Am A Mighty Woman Of Valour

Our prayer for you

Daddy-God, we pray over our lovely friend.

We ask that you bless her Lord for partnering with our organisation, *Mighty Woman of Valour.*

Help keep her thoughts aligned with Your Word and give her a hunger and a thirst to dig deeper into Your letter of love to us.

We pray for wisdom and discernment for every decision she makes and understanding for every answer she receives.

As she enters this day, may she know that Your mercies are new every morning and that Your grace is sufficient for anything she may face today. Remind her that she is an overcomer in Christ and deeply loved by You.

Today is a fresh new start and we thank you Holy Spirit that You will guide her into all Truth. Restore her soul as You lead her beside still waters and make her lie down in green pastures and give her rest even amidst chaos. May she experience Your everlasting peace every moment of every day.

We pray for uncommon favour with man, and as Your child, we know she already has favour with You. Thank you Father.

May she be successful at all she does and use her God-given gifts diligently to impact the world for You.

Thank you for protecting her and her family and thank you for providing for them. She walks in abundance and lacks nothing.

Because You are a good Father and You reward us for diligently seeking after You, we thank you Lord that she is blessed and that You can and will do exceedingly, abundantly and above all that she can ever ask or even think.

Holy are You Lord, and Your mercy endures forever.

We pray this in the precious name of Jesus
Amen!

Lots of love

Team MWOV

MWOV
MIGHTY WOMAN OF VALOUR

www.mightywomanofvalour.com

Daily Affirmation of Truth

There is only One Unique Me.
I am Fully Pleasing,
Entirely Accepted,
Unconditionally Forgiven
and Deeply Loved by God,
my Creator, Father,
Saviour & Lord.

I am Grateful for All that I Have
and Will Accomplish in the
Future through His Grace.

I Am Blessed!

10 NAMES OF GOD

ADONAI
Meaning: The Lord, My Great Lord
Scripture ref: Psalm 8; Habakkuk 3:19; Isa 40:3-5

EL ELYON
Meaning: God Most High
Scripture ref: Gen 14:17-22; Dan 4:34; Psalm 78:35

ELOHIM
Meaning: The All Powerful One ; The Creator of all things
Scripture ref: Genesis 1:1-3; Psalm 68; Deut 10:17

EL SHADDAI
Meaning: The Almighty God, The All Sufficient One
Scripture ref: Gen 17:1-3; Psalm 90:2; Gen 35:11

EMMANUEL / IMMANUEL
Meaning: God with us; Jesus was named Emmanuel / Immanuel
Scripture ref: Isa 7:14; Isa 8:8-10; Matt 1:23

JEHOVAH (YHWH / YHVH)
Meaning: "I AM" ; The One who Is (I AM, WHO I AM)
Scripture ref: Exo 3:14; Exo 6:2-4: Psalm 102

JEHOVAH JIREH
Meaning: The Lord, my Provider / The Lord will Provide
Scripture ref: Gen 22:13: Psalm 23: John 6:35

JEHOVAH RAPHA
Meaning: The Lord, my healer; The Lord who heals
Scripture ref: Exo 15: 25-27; Psalm 103:3; 1 Pet 2:24

JEHOVAH ROHI
Meaning: The Lord is My Shepherd
Scripture ref: Psalm 23:1-3; Heb 13:20; Rev 7:17

JEHOVAH SHALOM
Meaning: The Lord is Peace
Scripture ref: Num 6:22-27; Isa 9:6; Heb 13:20

Addresses & Contact Details

Name & Surname _____

Address: _____

_____

Number: _____

Mobile: _____

Email: _____

Website: _____

Birthday: _____

Notes: _____

Name & Surname _____

Address: _____

_____

Number: _____

Mobile: _____

Email: _____

Website: _____

Birthday: _____

Notes: _____

Addresses & Contact Details

Name & Surname _____

Address: _____

_____

Number: _____

Mobile: _____

Email: _____

Website: _____

Birthday: _____

Notes: _____

Name & Surname _____

Address: _____

_____

Number: _____

Mobile: _____

Email: _____

Website: _____

Birthday: _____

Notes: _____

DATE

SCHEDULE

6:00

7:00

8:00

9:00

10:00

11:00

12:00

1:00

2:00

3:00

4:00

5:00

6:00

7:00

8:00

9:00

GOALS

NOTES

√ TASKS

- ○
- ○
- ○
- ○
- ○
- ○
- ○
- ○
- ○
- ○
- ○
- ○
- ○
- ○
- ○
- ○

DATE

SCHEDULE

6:00

7:00

8:00

9:00

10:00

11:00

12:00

1:00

2:00

3:00

4:00

5:00

6:00

7:00

8:00

9:00

GOALS

NOTES

√ TASKS

- ○
- ○
- ○
- ○
- ○
- ○
- ○
- ○
- ○
- ○
- ○
- ○
- ○
- ○
- ○
- ○

DATE

SCHEDULE

6:00

7:00

8:00

9:00

10:00

11:00

12:00

1:00

2:00

3:00

4:00

5:00

6:00

7:00

8:00

9:00

GOALS

NOTES

√ TASKS

- ○
- ○
- ○
- ○
- ○
- ○
- ○
- ○
- ○
- ○
- ○
- ○
- ○
- ○
- ○
- ○

DATE

SCHEDULE

6:00

7:00

8:00

9:00

10:00

11:00

12:00

1:00

2:00

3:00

4:00

5:00

6:00

7:00

8:00

9:00

GOALS

NOTES

√ TASKS

○
○
○
○
○
○
○
○
○
○
○
○
○
○
○
○

DATE

SCHEDULE

6:00

7:00

8:00

9:00

10:00

11:00

12:00

1:00

2:00

3:00

4:00

5:00

6:00

7:00

8:00

9:00

GOALS

NOTES

√ TASKS

- ◯
- ◯
- ◯
- ◯
- ◯
- ◯
- ◯
- ◯
- ◯
- ◯
- ◯
- ◯
- ◯
- ◯
- ◯
- ◯

DATE

SCHEDULE

6:00

7:00

8:00

9:00

10:00

11:00

12:00

1:00

2:00

3:00

4:00

5:00

6:00

7:00

8:00

9:00

GOALS

NOTES

√ TASKS

- ○
- ○
- ○
- ○
- ○
- ○
- ○
- ○
- ○
- ○
- ○
- ○
- ○
- ○
- ○
- ○

DATE

SCHEDULE

6:00

7:00

8:00

9:00

10:00

11:00

12:00

1:00

2:00

3:00

4:00

5:00

6:00

7:00

8:00

9:00

GOALS

NOTES

✓ TASKS

- ○
- ○
- ○
- ○
- ○
- ○
- ○
- ○
- ○
- ○
- ○
- ○
- ○
- ○
- ○
- ○

DATE

SCHEDULE

6:00

7:00

8:00

9:00

10:00

11:00

12:00

1:00

2:00

3:00

4:00

5:00

6:00

7:00

8:00

9:00

GOALS

NOTES

√ TASKS

- ○
- ○
- ○
- ○
- ○
- ○
- ○
- ○
- ○
- ○
- ○
- ○
- ○
- ○
- ○
- ○

DATE

SCHEDULE

6:00

7:00

8:00

9:00

10:00

11:00

12:00

1:00

2:00

3:00

4:00

5:00

6:00

7:00

8:00

9:00

GOALS

NOTES

✓ TASKS

- ○ _____
- ○ _____
- ○ _____
- ○ _____
- ○ _____
- ○ _____
- ○ _____
- ○ _____
- ○ _____
- ○ _____
- ○ _____
- ○ _____
- ○ _____
- ○ _____
- ○ _____

DATE

SCHEDULE

6:00

7:00

8:00

9:00

10:00

11:00

12:00

1:00

2:00

3:00

4:00

5:00

6:00

7:00

8:00

9:00

GOALS

√ TASKS

○ _____

○ _____

○ _____

○ _____

○ _____

○ _____

○ _____

NOTES

○ _____

○ _____

○ _____

○ _____

○ _____

○ _____

○ _____

○ _____

○ _____

DATE

SCHEDULE

6:00

7:00

8:00

9:00

10:00

11:00

12:00

1:00

2:00

3:00

4:00

5:00

6:00

7:00

8:00

9:00

GOALS

NOTES

√ TASKS

- ◯
- ◯
- ◯
- ◯
- ◯
- ◯
- ◯
- ◯
- ◯
- ◯
- ◯
- ◯
- ◯
- ◯
- ◯
- ◯

DATE

SCHEDULE

6:00

7:00

8:00

9:00

10:00

11:00

12:00

1:00

2:00

3:00

4:00

5:00

6:00

7:00

8:00

9:00

GOALS

NOTES

√ **TASKS**

- ○ _____
- ○ _____
- ○ _____
- ○ _____
- ○ _____
- ○ _____
- ○ _____
- ○ _____
- ○ _____
- ○ _____
- ○ _____
- ○ _____
- ○ _____
- ○ _____
- ○ _____
- ○ _____
- ○ _____

DATE

SCHEDULE

6:00

7:00

8:00

9:00

10:00

11:00

12:00

1:00

2:00

3:00

4:00

5:00

6:00

7:00

8:00

9:00

GOALS

NOTES

√ TASKS

- ○
- ○
- ○
- ○
- ○
- ○
- ○
- ○
- ○
- ○
- ○
- ○
- ○
- ○
- ○
- ○

DATE

SCHEDULE

6:00

7:00

8:00

9:00

10:00

11:00

12:00

1:00

2:00

3:00

4:00

5:00

6:00

7:00

8:00

9:00

GOALS

NOTES

√ TASKS

○ _____
○ _____
○ _____
○ _____
○ _____
○ _____
○ _____
○ _____
○ _____
○ _____
○ _____
○ _____
○ _____
○ _____
○ _____
○ _____

DATE

SCHEDULE

6:00

7:00

8:00

9:00

10:00

11:00

12:00

1:00

2:00

3:00

4:00

5:00

6:00

7:00

8:00

9:00

GOALS

NOTES

√ **TASKS**

○ _____
○ _____
○ _____
○ _____
○ _____
○ _____
○ _____
○ _____
○ _____
○ _____
○ _____
○ _____
○ _____
○ _____
○ _____
○ _____

DATE

SCHEDULE

6:00

7:00

8:00

9:00

10:00

11:00

12:00

1:00

2:00

3:00

4:00

5:00

6:00

7:00

8:00

9:00

GOALS

NOTES

√ TASKS

- ○
- ○
- ○
- ○
- ○
- ○
- ○
- ○
- ○
- ○
- ○
- ○
- ○
- ○
- ○
- ○

DATE

SCHEDULE

6:00

7:00

8:00

9:00

10:00

11:00

12:00

1:00

2:00

3:00

4:00

5:00

6:00

7:00

8:00

9:00

GOALS

NOTES

✓ TASKS

- ○ _____
- ○ _____
- ○ _____
- ○ _____
- ○ _____
- ○ _____
- ○ _____
- ○ _____
- ○ _____
- ○ _____
- ○ _____
- ○ _____
- ○ _____
- ○ _____
- ○ _____
- ○ _____

DATE

SCHEDULE

6:00

7:00

8:00

9:00

10:00

11:00

12:00

1:00

2:00

3:00

4:00

5:00

6:00

7:00

8:00

9:00

GOALS

NOTES

√ TASKS

- ○
- ○
- ○
- ○
- ○
- ○
- ○
- ○
- ○
- ○
- ○
- ○
- ○
- ○
- ○
- ○

DATE

SCHEDULE

6:00

7:00

8:00

9:00

10:00

11:00

12:00

1:00

2:00

3:00

4:00

5:00

6:00

7:00

8:00

9:00

GOALS

NOTES

√ TASKS

- ○
- ○
- ○
- ○
- ○
- ○
- ○
- ○
- ○
- ○
- ○
- ○
- ○
- ○
- ○
- ○

DATE

SCHEDULE

6:00

7:00

8:00

9:00

10:00

11:00

12:00

1:00

2:00

3:00

4:00

5:00

6:00

7:00

8:00

9:00

GOALS

NOTES

√ TASKS

- ○
- ○
- ○
- ○
- ○
- ○
- ○
- ○
- ○
- ○
- ○
- ○
- ○
- ○
- ○
- ○
- ○

DATE

SCHEDULE

6:00

7:00

8:00

9:00

10:00

11:00

12:00

1:00

2:00

3:00

4:00

5:00

6:00

7:00

8:00

9:00

GOALS

NOTES

√ TASKS

- ○
- ○
- ○
- ○
- ○
- ○
- ○
- ○
- ○
- ○
- ○
- ○
- ○
- ○
- ○
- ○

DATE

SCHEDULE

6:00

7:00

8:00

9:00

10:00

11:00

12:00

1:00

2:00

3:00

4:00

5:00

6:00

7:00

8:00

9:00

GOALS

NOTES

✓ TASKS

- ◯ _____
- ◯ _____
- ◯ _____
- ◯ _____
- ◯ _____
- ◯ _____
- ◯ _____
- ◯ _____
- ◯ _____
- ◯ _____
- ◯ _____
- ◯ _____
- ◯ _____
- ◯ _____
- ◯ _____
- ◯ _____

DATE

SCHEDULE

6:00

7:00

8:00

9:00

10:00

11:00

12:00

1:00

2:00

3:00

4:00

5:00

6:00

7:00

8:00

9:00

GOALS

NOTES

√ TASKS

- ◯
- ◯
- ◯
- ◯
- ◯
- ◯
- ◯
- ◯
- ◯
- ◯
- ◯
- ◯
- ◯
- ◯
- ◯
- ◯

DATE

SCHEDULE

6:00

7:00

8:00

9:00

10:00

11:00

12:00

1:00

2:00

3:00

4:00

5:00

6:00

7:00

8:00

9:00

GOALS

NOTES

√ TASKS

- ○ _____
- ○ _____
- ○ _____
- ○ _____
- ○ _____
- ○ _____
- ○ _____
- ○ _____
- ○ _____
- ○ _____
- ○ _____
- ○ _____
- ○ _____
- ○ _____
- ○ _____
- ○ _____

DATE

SCHEDULE

6:00

7:00

8:00

9:00

10:00

11:00

12:00

1:00

2:00

3:00

4:00

5:00

6:00

7:00

8:00

9:00

GOALS

NOTES

√ **TASKS**

- ○
- ○
- ○
- ○
- ○
- ○
- ○
- ○
- ○
- ○
- ○
- ○
- ○
- ○
- ○
- ○

DATE

SCHEDULE

6:00

7:00

8:00

9:00

10:00

11:00

12:00

1:00

2:00

3:00

4:00

5:00

6:00

7:00

8:00

9:00

GOALS

NOTES

√ TASKS

○ _____

○ _____

○ _____

○ _____

○ _____

○ _____

○ _____

○ _____

○ _____

○ _____

○ _____

○ _____

○ _____

○ _____

○ _____

○ _____

DATE

SCHEDULE

6:00

7:00

8:00

9:00

10:00

11:00

12:00

1:00

2:00

3:00

4:00

5:00

6:00

7:00

8:00

9:00

GOALS

NOTES

✓ TASKS

- ○ _____
- ○ _____
- ○ _____
- ○ _____
- ○ _____
- ○ _____
- ○ _____
- ○ _____
- ○ _____
- ○ _____
- ○ _____
- ○ _____
- ○ _____
- ○ _____
- ○ _____
- ○ _____

DATE

SCHEDULE

6:00

7:00

8:00

9:00

10:00

11:00

12:00

1:00

2:00

3:00

4:00

5:00

6:00

7:00

8:00

9:00

GOALS

NOTES

✓ TASKS

- ◯
- ◯
- ◯
- ◯
- ◯
- ◯
- ◯
- ◯
- ◯
- ◯
- ◯
- ◯
- ◯
- ◯
- ◯
- ◯

DATE

SCHEDULE

6:00

7:00

8:00

9:00

10:00

11:00

12:00

1:00

2:00

3:00

4:00

5:00

6:00

7:00

8:00

9:00

GOALS

NOTES

✓ TASKS

- ○
- ○
- ○
- ○
- ○
- ○
- ○
- ○
- ○
- ○
- ○
- ○
- ○
- ○
- ○
- ○

DATE

SCHEDULE

6:00

7:00

8:00

9:00

10:00

11:00

12:00

1:00

2:00

3:00

4:00

5:00

6:00

7:00

8:00

9:00

GOALS

NOTES

✓ TASKS

- ○ _____
- ○ _____
- ○ _____
- ○ _____
- ○ _____
- ○ _____
- ○ _____
- ○ _____
- ○ _____
- ○ _____
- ○ _____
- ○ _____
- ○ _____
- ○ _____
- ○ _____
- ○ _____

DATE

SCHEDULE

6:00

7:00

8:00

9:00

10:00

11:00

12:00

1:00

2:00

3:00

4:00

5:00

6:00

7:00

8:00

9:00

GOALS

NOTES

✓ TASKS

- ○
- ○
- ○
- ○
- ○
- ○
- ○
- ○
- ○
- ○
- ○
- ○
- ○
- ○
- ○
- ○

DATE

SCHEDULE

6:00

7:00

8:00

9:00

10:00

11:00

12:00

1:00

2:00

3:00

4:00

5:00

6:00

7:00

8:00

9:00

GOALS

NOTES

√ TASKS

○
○
○
○
○
○
○
○
○
○
○
○
○
○
○
○

DATE

SCHEDULE

6:00

7:00

8:00

9:00

10:00

11:00

12:00

1:00

2:00

3:00

4:00

5:00

6:00

7:00

8:00

9:00

GOALS

NOTES

√ TASKS

- ○
- ○
- ○
- ○
- ○
- ○
- ○
- ○
- ○
- ○
- ○
- ○
- ○
- ○
- ○
- ○

DATE

SCHEDULE

6:00

7:00

8:00

9:00

10:00

11:00

12:00

1:00

2:00

3:00

4:00

5:00

6:00

7:00

8:00

9:00

GOALS

NOTES

√ TASKS

- ◯
- ◯
- ◯
- ◯
- ◯
- ◯
- ◯
- ◯
- ◯
- ◯
- ◯
- ◯
- ◯
- ◯
- ◯
- ◯

DATE

SCHEDULE

6:00

7:00

8:00

9:00

10:00

11:00

12:00

1:00

2:00

3:00

4:00

5:00

6:00

7:00

8:00

9:00

GOALS

NOTES

√ TASKS

- ○
- ○
- ○
- ○
- ○
- ○
- ○
- ○
- ○
- ○
- ○
- ○
- ○
- ○
- ○
- ○

DATE

SCHEDULE

6:00

7:00

8:00

9:00

10:00

11:00

12:00

1:00

2:00

3:00

4:00

5:00

6:00

7:00

8:00

9:00

GOALS

NOTES

✓ TASKS

- ○ _____
- ○ _____
- ○ _____
- ○ _____
- ○ _____
- ○ _____
- ○ _____
- ○ _____
- ○ _____
- ○ _____
- ○ _____
- ○ _____
- ○ _____
- ○ _____
- ○ _____
- ○ _____

DATE

SCHEDULE

6:00

7:00

8:00

9:00

10:00

11:00

12:00

1:00

2:00

3:00

4:00

5:00

6:00

7:00

8:00

9:00

GOALS

NOTES

√ TASKS

- ○
- ○
- ○
- ○
- ○
- ○
- ○
- ○
- ○
- ○
- ○
- ○
- ○
- ○
- ○
- ○

DATE

SCHEDULE

6:00

7:00

8:00

9:00

10:00

11:00

12:00

1:00

2:00

3:00

4:00

5:00

6:00

7:00

8:00

9:00

GOALS

NOTES

√ TASKS

- ◯
- ◯
- ◯
- ◯
- ◯
- ◯
- ◯
- ◯
- ◯
- ◯
- ◯
- ◯
- ◯
- ◯
- ◯
- ◯

DATE

SCHEDULE

6:00

7:00

8:00

9:00

10:00

11:00

12:00

1:00

2:00

3:00

4:00

5:00

6:00

7:00

8:00

9:00

GOALS

NOTES

√ TASKS

○ _____
○ _____
○ _____
○ _____
○ _____
○ _____
○ _____
○ _____
○ _____
○ _____
○ _____
○ _____
○ _____
○ _____
○ _____
○ _____
○ _____

DATE

SCHEDULE

6:00

7:00

8:00

9:00

10:00

11:00

12:00

1:00

2:00

3:00

4:00

5:00

6:00

7:00

8:00

9:00

GOALS

NOTES

√ TASKS

- ○
- ○
- ○
- ○
- ○
- ○
- ○
- ○
- ○
- ○
- ○
- ○
- ○
- ○
- ○
- ○

DATE

SCHEDULE

6:00

7:00

8:00

9:00

10:00

11:00

12:00

1:00

2:00

3:00

4:00

5:00

6:00

7:00

8:00

9:00

GOALS

NOTES

√ TASKS

- ○
- ○
- ○
- ○
- ○
- ○
- ○
- ○
- ○
- ○
- ○
- ○
- ○
- ○
- ○
- ○
- ○

DATE

SCHEDULE

6:00

7:00

8:00

9:00

10:00

11:00

12:00

1:00

2:00

3:00

4:00

5:00

6:00

7:00

8:00

9:00

GOALS

NOTES

✓ TASKS

- ○
- ○
- ○
- ○
- ○
- ○
- ○
- ○
- ○
- ○
- ○
- ○
- ○
- ○
- ○
- ○

DATE

SCHEDULE

6:00

7:00

8:00

9:00

10:00

11:00

12:00

1:00

2:00

3:00

4:00

5:00

6:00

7:00

8:00

9:00

GOALS

NOTES

√ TASKS

DATE

SCHEDULE

6:00

7:00

8:00

9:00

10:00

11:00

12:00

1:00

2:00

3:00

4:00

5:00

6:00

7:00

8:00

9:00

GOALS

NOTES

√ TASKS

- ◯
- ◯
- ◯
- ◯
- ◯
- ◯
- ◯
- ◯
- ◯
- ◯
- ◯
- ◯
- ◯
- ◯
- ◯
- ◯

DATE

SCHEDULE

6:00

7:00

8:00

9:00

10:00

11:00

12:00

1:00

2:00

3:00

4:00

5:00

6:00

7:00

8:00

9:00

GOALS

NOTES

√ TASKS

- ○
- ○
- ○
- ○
- ○
- ○
- ○
- ○
- ○
- ○
- ○
- ○
- ○
- ○
- ○
- ○

DATE

SCHEDULE

6:00

7:00

8:00

9:00

10:00

11:00

12:00

1:00

2:00

3:00

4:00

5:00

6:00

7:00

8:00

9:00

GOALS

NOTES

√ TASKS

- ○ _____
- ○ _____
- ○ _____
- ○ _____
- ○ _____
- ○ _____
- ○ _____
- ○ _____
- ○ _____
- ○ _____
- ○ _____
- ○ _____
- ○ _____
- ○ _____
- ○ _____
- ○ _____

DATE

SCHEDULE

6:00

7:00

8:00

9:00

10:00

11:00

12:00

1:00

2:00

3:00

4:00

5:00

6:00

7:00

8:00

9:00

GOALS

NOTES

√ TASKS

- ○
- ○
- ○
- ○
- ○
- ○
- ○
- ○
- ○
- ○
- ○
- ○
- ○
- ○
- ○
- ○

DATE

SCHEDULE

6:00

7:00

8:00

9:00

10:00

11:00

12:00

1:00

2:00

3:00

4:00

5:00

6:00

7:00

8:00

9:00

GOALS

NOTES

√ TASKS

- ○
- ○
- ○
- ○
- ○
- ○
- ○
- ○
- ○
- ○
- ○
- ○
- ○
- ○
- ○
- ○
- ○

DATE

SCHEDULE

6:00

7:00

8:00

9:00

10:00

11:00

12:00

1:00

2:00

3:00

4:00

5:00

6:00

7:00

8:00

9:00

GOALS

NOTES

√ TASKS

- ○
- ○
- ○
- ○
- ○
- ○
- ○
- ○
- ○
- ○
- ○
- ○
- ○
- ○
- ○
- ○

DATE

SCHEDULE

6:00

7:00

8:00

9:00

10:00

11:00

12:00

1:00

2:00

3:00

4:00

5:00

6:00

7:00

8:00

9:00

GOALS

NOTES

✓ TASKS

- ◯
- ◯
- ◯
- ◯
- ◯
- ◯
- ◯
- ◯
- ◯
- ◯
- ◯
- ◯
- ◯
- ◯
- ◯
- ◯

DATE

SCHEDULE

6:00

7:00

8:00

9:00

10:00

11:00

12:00

1:00

2:00

3:00

4:00

5:00

6:00

7:00

8:00

9:00

GOALS

NOTES

✓ TASKS

- ○
- ○
- ○
- ○
- ○
- ○
- ○
- ○
- ○
- ○
- ○
- ○
- ○
- ○
- ○
- ○

DATE

SCHEDULE

6:00

7:00

8:00

9:00

10:00

11:00

12:00

1:00

2:00

3:00

4:00

5:00

6:00

7:00

8:00

9:00

GOALS

NOTES

√ TASKS

- ○ _____
- ○ _____
- ○ _____
- ○ _____
- ○ _____
- ○ _____
- ○ _____
- ○ _____
- ○ _____
- ○ _____
- ○ _____
- ○ _____
- ○ _____
- ○ _____
- ○ _____
- ○ _____

DATE

SCHEDULE

6:00

7:00

8:00

9:00

10:00

11:00

12:00

1:00

2:00

3:00

4:00

5:00

6:00

7:00

8:00

9:00

GOALS

NOTES

√ TASKS

- ○ _____
- ○ _____
- ○ _____
- ○ _____
- ○ _____
- ○ _____
- ○ _____
- ○ _____
- ○ _____
- ○ _____
- ○ _____
- ○ _____
- ○ _____
- ○ _____
- ○ _____
- ○ _____

DATE

SCHEDULE

6:00

7:00

8:00

9:00

10:00

11:00

12:00

1:00

2:00

3:00

4:00

5:00

6:00

7:00

8:00

9:00

GOALS

NOTES

√ TASKS

○

○

○

○

○

○

○

○

○

○

○

○

○

○

○

○

DATE

SCHEDULE

6:00

7:00

8:00

9:00

10:00

11:00

12:00

1:00

2:00

3:00

4:00

5:00

6:00

7:00

8:00

9:00

GOALS

NOTES

√ TASKS

- ○
- ○
- ○
- ○
- ○
- ○
- ○
- ○
- ○
- ○
- ○
- ○
- ○
- ○
- ○
- ○

DATE

SCHEDULE

6:00

7:00

8:00

9:00

10:00

11:00

12:00

1:00

2:00

3:00

4:00

5:00

6:00

7:00

8:00

9:00

GOALS

NOTES

√ TASKS

- ◯
- ◯
- ◯
- ◯
- ◯
- ◯
- ◯
- ◯
- ◯
- ◯
- ◯
- ◯
- ◯
- ◯
- ◯
- ◯

DATE

SCHEDULE

6:00

7:00

8:00

9:00

10:00

11:00

12:00

1:00

2:00

3:00

4:00

5:00

6:00

7:00

8:00

9:00

GOALS

NOTES

√ TASKS

DATE

SCHEDULE

6:00

7:00

8:00

9:00

10:00

11:00

12:00

1:00

2:00

3:00

4:00

5:00

6:00

7:00

8:00

9:00

GOALS

NOTES

√ TASKS

○ _____
○ _____
○ _____
○ _____
○ _____
○ _____
○ _____
○ _____
○ _____
○ _____
○ _____
○ _____
○ _____
○ _____
○ _____
○ _____

DATE

SCHEDULE

6:00

7:00

8:00

9:00

10:00

11:00

12:00

1:00

2:00

3:00

4:00

5:00

6:00

7:00

8:00

9:00

GOALS

NOTES

✓ TASKS

- ○ _____
- ○ _____
- ○ _____
- ○ _____
- ○ _____
- ○ _____
- ○ _____
- ○ _____
- ○ _____
- ○ _____
- ○ _____
- ○ _____
- ○ _____
- ○ _____
- ○ _____
- ○ _____

DATE

SCHEDULE

6:00

7:00

8:00

9:00

10:00

11:00

12:00

1:00

2:00

3:00

4:00

5:00

6:00

7:00

8:00

9:00

GOALS

NOTES

✓ TASKS

○ _____
○ _____
○ _____
○ _____
○ _____
○ _____
○ _____
○ _____
○ _____
○ _____
○ _____
○ _____
○ _____
○ _____
○ _____
○ _____

DATE

SCHEDULE

6:00

7:00

8:00

9:00

10:00

11:00

12:00

1:00

2:00

3:00

4:00

5:00

6:00

7:00

8:00

9:00

GOALS

NOTES

✓ TASKS

- ○ _____
- ○ _____
- ○ _____
- ○ _____
- ○ _____
- ○ _____
- ○ _____
- ○ _____
- ○ _____
- ○ _____
- ○ _____
- ○ _____
- ○ _____
- ○ _____
- ○ _____
- ○ _____

DATE

SCHEDULE

6:00

7:00

8:00

9:00

10:00

11:00

12:00

1:00

2:00

3:00

4:00

5:00

6:00

7:00

8:00

9:00

GOALS

NOTES

√ TASKS

○ _____
○ _____
○ _____
○ _____
○ _____
○ _____
○ _____
○ _____
○ _____
○ _____
○ _____
○ _____
○ _____
○ _____
○ _____
○ _____

DATE

SCHEDULE

6:00

7:00

8:00

9:00

10:00

11:00

12:00

1:00

2:00

3:00

4:00

5:00

6:00

7:00

8:00

9:00

GOALS

NOTES

√ TASKS

- ○ _____
- ○ _____
- ○ _____
- ○ _____
- ○ _____
- ○ _____
- ○ _____
- ○ _____
- ○ _____
- ○ _____
- ○ _____
- ○ _____
- ○ _____
- ○ _____
- ○ _____
- ○ _____

DATE

SCHEDULE

6:00

7:00

8:00

9:00

10:00

11:00

12:00

1:00

2:00

3:00

4:00

5:00

6:00

7:00

8:00

9:00

GOALS

NOTES

√ TASKS

- ○ _____
- ○ _____
- ○ _____
- ○ _____
- ○ _____
- ○ _____
- ○ _____
- ○ _____
- ○ _____
- ○ _____
- ○ _____
- ○ _____
- ○ _____
- ○ _____
- ○ _____
- ○ _____

DATE

SCHEDULE

6:00

7:00

8:00

9:00

10:00

11:00

12:00

1:00

2:00

3:00

4:00

5:00

6:00

7:00

8:00

9:00

GOALS

NOTES

√ TASKS

- ○
- ○
- ○
- ○
- ○
- ○
- ○
- ○
- ○
- ○
- ○
- ○
- ○
- ○
- ○
- ○

DATE

SCHEDULE

6:00

7:00

8:00

9:00

10:00

11:00

12:00

1:00

2:00

3:00

4:00

5:00

6:00

7:00

8:00

9:00

GOALS

NOTES

√ TASKS

- ○
- ○
- ○
- ○
- ○
- ○
- ○
- ○
- ○
- ○
- ○
- ○
- ○
- ○
- ○
- ○

DATE

SCHEDULE

6:00

7:00

8:00

9:00

10:00

11:00

12:00

1:00

2:00

3:00

4:00

5:00

6:00

7:00

8:00

9:00

GOALS

NOTES

✓ TASKS

- ○ _____
- ○ _____
- ○ _____
- ○ _____
- ○ _____
- ○ _____
- ○ _____
- ○ _____
- ○ _____
- ○ _____
- ○ _____
- ○ _____
- ○ _____
- ○ _____
- ○ _____
- ○ _____

DATE

SCHEDULE

6:00

7:00

8:00

9:00

10:00

11:00

12:00

1:00

2:00

3:00

4:00

5:00

6:00

7:00

8:00

9:00

GOALS

NOTES

✓ TASKS

- ○
- ○
- ○
- ○
- ○
- ○
- ○
- ○
- ○
- ○
- ○
- ○
- ○
- ○
- ○
- ○

DATE

SCHEDULE

6:00

7:00

8:00

9:00

10:00

11:00

12:00

1:00

2:00

3:00

4:00

5:00

6:00

7:00

8:00

9:00

GOALS

NOTES

√ TASKS

- ○
- ○
- ○
- ○
- ○
- ○
- ○
- ○
- ○
- ○
- ○
- ○
- ○
- ○
- ○
- ○

DATE

SCHEDULE

6:00

7:00

8:00

9:00

10:00

11:00

12:00

1:00

2:00

3:00

4:00

5:00

6:00

7:00

8:00

9:00

GOALS

NOTES

√ TASKS

- ○
- ○
- ○
- ○
- ○
- ○
- ○
- ○
- ○
- ○
- ○
- ○
- ○
- ○
- ○
- ○

DATE

SCHEDULE

6:00

7:00

8:00

9:00

10:00

11:00

12:00

1:00

2:00

3:00

4:00

5:00

6:00

7:00

8:00

9:00

GOALS

NOTES

√ TASKS

- ○
- ○
- ○
- ○
- ○
- ○
- ○
- ○
- ○
- ○
- ○
- ○
- ○
- ○
- ○
- ○

DATE

SCHEDULE

6:00

7:00

8:00

9:00

10:00

11:00

12:00

1:00

2:00

3:00

4:00

5:00

6:00

7:00

8:00

9:00

GOALS

NOTES

√ TASKS

○
○
○
○
○
○
○
○
○
○
○
○
○
○
○
○

DATE

SCHEDULE

6:00

7:00

8:00

9:00

10:00

11:00

12:00

1:00

2:00

3:00

4:00

5:00

6:00

7:00

8:00

9:00

GOALS

NOTES

√ TASKS

- ○
- ○
- ○
- ○
- ○
- ○
- ○
- ○
- ○
- ○
- ○
- ○
- ○
- ○
- ○
- ○

DATE

SCHEDULE

6:00

7:00

8:00

9:00

10:00

11:00

12:00

1:00

2:00

3:00

4:00

5:00

6:00

7:00

8:00

9:00

GOALS

NOTES

√ TASKS

- ◯
- ◯
- ◯
- ◯
- ◯
- ◯
- ◯
- ◯
- ◯
- ◯
- ◯
- ◯
- ◯
- ◯
- ◯
- ◯

DATE

SCHEDULE

6:00

7:00

8:00

9:00

10:00

11:00

12:00

1:00

2:00

3:00

4:00

5:00

6:00

7:00

8:00

9:00

GOALS

NOTES

√ TASKS

○ _____
○ _____
○ _____
○ _____
○ _____
○ _____
○ _____
○ _____
○ _____
○ _____
○ _____
○ _____
○ _____
○ _____
○ _____
○ _____

DATE

SCHEDULE

6:00

7:00

8:00

9:00

10:00

11:00

12:00

1:00

2:00

3:00

4:00

5:00

6:00

7:00

8:00

9:00

GOALS

NOTES

√ TASKS

- ○
- ○
- ○
- ○
- ○
- ○
- ○
- ○
- ○
- ○
- ○
- ○
- ○
- ○
- ○
- ○

DATE

SCHEDULE

6:00

7:00

8:00

9:00

10:00

11:00

12:00

1:00

2:00

3:00

4:00

5:00

6:00

7:00

8:00

9:00

GOALS

NOTES

√ TASKS

- ○ _____
- ○ _____
- ○ _____
- ○ _____
- ○ _____
- ○ _____
- ○ _____
- ○ _____
- ○ _____
- ○ _____
- ○ _____
- ○ _____
- ○ _____
- ○ _____
- ○ _____
- ○ _____

DATE

SCHEDULE

6:00

7:00

8:00

9:00

10:00

11:00

12:00

1:00

2:00

3:00

4:00

5:00

6:00

7:00

8:00

9:00

GOALS

NOTES

√ TASKS

○
○
○
○
○
○
○
○
○
○
○
○
○
○
○
○

DATE

SCHEDULE

6:00

7:00

8:00

9:00

10:00

11:00

12:00

1:00

2:00

3:00

4:00

5:00

6:00

7:00

8:00

9:00

GOALS

NOTES

✓ TASKS

○ _____
○ _____
○ _____
○ _____
○ _____
○ _____
○ _____
○ _____
○ _____
○ _____
○ _____
○ _____
○ _____
○ _____
○ _____
○ _____

DATE

SCHEDULE

6:00

7:00

8:00

9:00

10:00

11:00

12:00

1:00

2:00

3:00

4:00

5:00

6:00

7:00

8:00

9:00

GOALS

NOTES

√ TASKS

○
○
○
○
○
○
○
○
○
○
○
○
○
○
○
○

DATE

SCHEDULE

6:00

7:00

8:00

9:00

10:00

11:00

12:00

1:00

2:00

3:00

4:00

5:00

6:00

7:00

8:00

9:00

GOALS

NOTES

√ TASKS

○
○
○
○
○
○
○
○
○
○
○
○
○
○
○
○

DATE

SCHEDULE

6:00

7:00

8:00

9:00

10:00

11:00

12:00

1:00

2:00

3:00

4:00

5:00

6:00

7:00

8:00

9:00

GOALS

NOTES

√ TASKS

- ○
- ○
- ○
- ○
- ○
- ○
- ○
- ○
- ○
- ○
- ○
- ○
- ○
- ○
- ○
- ○

DATE

SCHEDULE

6:00

7:00

8:00

9:00

10:00

11:00

12:00

1:00

2:00

3:00

4:00

5:00

6:00

7:00

8:00

9:00

GOALS

NOTES

√ TASKS

- ◯
- ◯
- ◯
- ◯
- ◯
- ◯
- ◯
- ◯
- ◯
- ◯
- ◯
- ◯
- ◯
- ◯
- ◯
- ◯

DATE

SCHEDULE

6:00

7:00

8:00

9:00

10:00

11:00

12:00

1:00

2:00

3:00

4:00

5:00

6:00

7:00

8:00

9:00

GOALS

NOTES

√ TASKS

- ○
- ○
- ○
- ○
- ○
- ○
- ○
- ○
- ○
- ○
- ○
- ○
- ○
- ○
- ○
- ○
- ○

DATE

SCHEDULE

6:00

7:00

8:00

9:00

10:00

11:00

12:00

1:00

2:00

3:00

4:00

5:00

6:00

7:00

8:00

9:00

GOALS

NOTES

√ TASKS

- ○
- ○
- ○
- ○
- ○
- ○
- ○
- ○
- ○
- ○
- ○
- ○
- ○
- ○
- ○
- ○

DATE

SCHEDULE

6:00

7:00

8:00

9:00

10:00

11:00

12:00

1:00

2:00

3:00

4:00

5:00

6:00

7:00

8:00

9:00

GOALS

NOTES

✓ TASKS

- ○
- ○
- ○
- ○
- ○
- ○
- ○
- ○
- ○
- ○
- ○
- ○
- ○
- ○
- ○
- ○

DATE

SCHEDULE

6:00

7:00

8:00

9:00

10:00

11:00

12:00

1:00

2:00

3:00

4:00

5:00

6:00

7:00

8:00

9:00

GOALS

NOTES

✓ TASKS

- ○
- ○
- ○
- ○
- ○
- ○
- ○
- ○
- ○
- ○
- ○
- ○
- ○
- ○
- ○
- ○

DATE

SCHEDULE

6:00

7:00

8:00

9:00

10:00

11:00

12:00

1:00

2:00

3:00

4:00

5:00

6:00

7:00

8:00

9:00

GOALS

NOTES

✓ TASKS

- ○
- ○
- ○
- ○
- ○
- ○
- ○
- ○
- ○
- ○
- ○
- ○
- ○
- ○
- ○
- ○
- ○

DATE

SCHEDULE

6:00

7:00

8:00

9:00

10:00

11:00

12:00

1:00

2:00

3:00

4:00

5:00

6:00

7:00

8:00

9:00

GOALS

NOTES

✓ TASKS

- ○ _____
- ○ _____
- ○ _____
- ○ _____
- ○ _____
- ○ _____
- ○ _____
- ○ _____
- ○ _____
- ○ _____
- ○ _____
- ○ _____
- ○ _____
- ○ _____
- ○ _____
- ○ _____

DATE

SCHEDULE

6:00

7:00

8:00

9:00

10:00

11:00

12:00

1:00

2:00

3:00

4:00

5:00

6:00

7:00

8:00

9:00

GOALS

NOTES

✓ TASKS

- ○
- ○
- ○
- ○
- ○
- ○
- ○
- ○
- ○
- ○
- ○
- ○
- ○
- ○
- ○
- ○

DATE

SCHEDULE

6:00

7:00

8:00

9:00

10:00

11:00

12:00

1:00

2:00

3:00

4:00

5:00

6:00

7:00

8:00

9:00

GOALS

NOTES

√ TASKS

- ○
- ○
- ○
- ○
- ○
- ○
- ○
- ○
- ○
- ○
- ○
- ○
- ○
- ○
- ○
- ○

DATE

SCHEDULE

6:00

7:00

8:00

9:00

10:00

11:00

12:00

1:00

2:00

3:00

4:00

5:00

6:00

7:00

8:00

9:00

GOALS

NOTES

√ TASKS

○
○
○
○
○
○
○
○
○
○
○
○
○
○
○
○

DATE

SCHEDULE

6:00

7:00

8:00

9:00

10:00

11:00

12:00

1:00

2:00

3:00

4:00

5:00

6:00

7:00

8:00

9:00

GOALS

NOTES

√ TASKS

- ○
- ○
- ○
- ○
- ○
- ○
- ○
- ○
- ○
- ○
- ○
- ○
- ○
- ○
- ○
- ○
- ○

DATE

SCHEDULE

6:00

7:00

8:00

9:00

10:00

11:00

12:00

1:00

2:00

3:00

4:00

5:00

6:00

7:00

8:00

9:00

GOALS

NOTES

√ TASKS

- ○
- ○
- ○
- ○
- ○
- ○
- ○
- ○
- ○
- ○
- ○
- ○
- ○
- ○
- ○

DATE

SCHEDULE

6:00

7:00

8:00

9:00

10:00

11:00

12:00

1:00

2:00

3:00

4:00

5:00

6:00

7:00

8:00

9:00

GOALS

NOTES

✓ TASKS

- ○
- ○
- ○
- ○
- ○
- ○
- ○
- ○
- ○
- ○
- ○
- ○
- ○
- ○
- ○

DATE

SCHEDULE

6:00

7:00

8:00

9:00

10:00

11:00

12:00

1:00

2:00

3:00

4:00

5:00

6:00

7:00

8:00

9:00

GOALS

NOTES

✓ TASKS

- ○
- ○
- ○
- ○
- ○
- ○
- ○
- ○
- ○
- ○
- ○
- ○
- ○
- ○
- ○
- ○

DATE

SCHEDULE

6:00

7:00

8:00

9:00

10:00

11:00

12:00

1:00

2:00

3:00

4:00

5:00

6:00

7:00

8:00

9:00

GOALS

NOTES

√ TASKS

- ○
- ○
- ○
- ○
- ○
- ○
- ○
- ○
- ○
- ○
- ○
- ○
- ○
- ○
- ○
- ○

DATE

SCHEDULE

6:00

7:00

8:00

9:00

10:00

11:00

12:00

1:00

2:00

3:00

4:00

5:00

6:00

7:00

8:00

9:00

GOALS

NOTES

✓ TASKS

- ○ _____
- ○ _____
- ○ _____
- ○ _____
- ○ _____
- ○ _____
- ○ _____
- ○ _____
- ○ _____
- ○ _____
- ○ _____
- ○ _____
- ○ _____
- ○ _____
- ○ _____

DATE

SCHEDULE

6:00

7:00

8:00

9:00

10:00

11:00

12:00

1:00

2:00

3:00

4:00

5:00

6:00

7:00

8:00

9:00

GOALS

NOTES

√ TASKS

- ○
- ○
- ○
- ○
- ○
- ○
- ○
- ○
- ○
- ○
- ○
- ○
- ○
- ○
- ○
- ○

DATE

SCHEDULE

6:00

7:00

8:00

9:00

10:00

11:00

12:00

1:00

2:00

3:00

4:00

5:00

6:00

7:00

8:00

9:00

GOALS

NOTES

√ TASKS

- ◯ _____
- ◯ _____
- ◯ _____
- ◯ _____
- ◯ _____
- ◯ _____
- ◯ _____
- ◯ _____
- ◯ _____
- ◯ _____
- ◯ _____
- ◯ _____
- ◯ _____
- ◯ _____
- ◯ _____
- ◯ _____